D0860223

Tropical Cocktails

Tropical
Cocktails

by BARRY SHELBY
Principal photography by Kenneth Chen

a miniSeries book
Abbeville Press Publishers
New York London Paris

Contents

Introduction

Any mixed drink should be fun. The tropical cocktail, however, should be flamboyant, exuberant, totally shameless fun. While some cocktails—the Manhattan, say, or the Martini—suggest breeding and class, the tropical drink has nothing the least bit snooty about it. The names alone can be so utterly ridiculous that one has to laugh: "Swimming Ashore for the Songs of Sunrise" or "The Green-Tailed Dragon of the Maroon Morning"—to pinch two from Gary Regan's *The Bartender's Bible*.

Serious bartenders, specifically those who eschew the blender, will look down their swizzle sticks at many of the concoctions you will find here. But the tropical cocktail is often the people's choice—particularly among those who enjoy a good time. The modern mixed drink is largely a product of the Roaring Twenties, and its Golden Age ran the length of Prohibition, to be ended only by the onset of World War II. Many of the drinks in this volume, however, were popularized after the war, and they mirror a change in taste: they had no association with the upper class or exclusive country clubs, and their tropical nature reflected the postwar sense of freedom and ease of travel, whether to the Pacific Isles or other "exotic" locales. Although the classic cocktail has made a recent comeback, the genuine popularity of the tropical cocktail has never waned.

No precise criteria define tropical drinks, but most share some characteristics. They often include fruit flavorings and frequently feature garish garnishes. Often their portions are large and their effects potent. Some are blended with ice into a frosty slurry that necessitates using a straw. Their names evoke sultry equatorial settings.

Many tropical cocktails were invented by bartenders and restaurateurs—such as California's Victor "Trader Vic" Bergeron—who hoped to transport patrons to the exotic places suggested by the ingredients and monikers of the drinks they served: the Blue Hawaiian, the Mai Tai, the Zombie. The Mai Tai allegedly got its name from the reaction of two Tahitians who sampled it. As reported by Trader Vic, after drinking his creation, they cried out "Mai Tai—roe ae!" ("out of this world—the best," per Bergeron's translation).

Rum and tequila, both produced south of the border, are closely associated with tropical cocktails. They are so-called plant distillates (in contrast to grain-based spirits) and are the primary alcohol in several of the drink recipes that follow.

Rum

If gin is the central ingredient in many classic cocktails, rum is its esteemed and invaluable counterpart in the house of tropical drinks.

For all the woe that the arrival of Christopher Columbus inflicted on the native inhabitants of the Caribbean, his entourage can at least be credited with supplying sugarcane stock on their second visit, in 1493. The West Indies were thus blessed with a future filled with rum and the considerable fortunes it generated. For more than two hundred years rum has been widely consumed, and in fact it outsold gin in eighteenth-century England. It remains in fashion today: Bacardi rum is reputedly the best-selling spirit in the world.

One of rum's early nicknames was "Kill Devil." This came from the notion that rum was a cure for Satan's ills. During Prohibition, Bill McCoy transported rum from the Bahamas (where it was legally produced in His Majesty's Empire) to the "Rum Row" Channel off the coast of the U.S., where he sold it legally in international waters. Unlike some of the swill then being peddled to a dry and thirsty nation, his rum became gratefully known as "the real McCoy."

Mr. Boston's Official Bartender's and Party Guide says that rum is the drink of "romantics and adventurers." In some of its stronger incarnations, such as 151 proof, it is no doubt also the first choice of the alcoholically adventurous. But rum, for reasons quite apart from its punch, simply mixes well with the fruit juices, citruses, and sweeteners so often used to flavor tropical drinks. And so it is found in everything from Zombies to Piña Coladas, Daiquiris to Mai Tais—and much in between.

Initially, rum was the offspring of necessity: an attempt to deal with the vast but initially worthless

amounts of molasses syrup left behind in the production of granulated sugar. Someone astutely noticed that the molasses naturally fermented in bottles left under the Caribbean sun, and rum came to life. The modern rum-making process is one that involves two mysterious (and not entirely pleasant sounding) by-products of the initial distillation of sugarcane: "skimming" and "dunder." These are added to diluted sugarcane molasses before the rich brew is fermented and finally distilled into rum.

The cognoscenti can identify a range of rum flavors as numerous and varied as those of wine—apparently, it all depends on the method and mix of skimming, dunder, water, and molasses, as well as on the aging. For most of us, distinctions among rums are quite a bit simpler: There are light-bodied rums and heavy ones, marketed as white, gold, or dark. I will avoid the complexities of distillation and state simply that light rums are the product of efficient, modern continuous stills, whereas the heavy-bodied ones are the result of the more traditional pot still, which is less precise, scientifically speaking, but allows for more flavorful products.

White rums tend to be light bodied and are sold under brand names such as Bacardi and Ronrico. They are generally made in Puerto Rico, Trinidad, and Barbados. Best used as a mixer, white rum is charcoal filtered to remove impurities and aged, albeit briefly, in plain oak or steel casks. Golden rum, which has a bit more body and flavor, is generally aged for longer periods.

Dark varieties such as Myers's and Captain Morgan are full bodied and, indeed, more traditional. Unlike white rum, which is made using the continuous still, dark rum is produced the old-fashioned way, in a pot still. It is aged, sometimes as long as twenty years, in oak casks that have been charred. Sometimes more syrup is added to increase body and flavor. Dark rum hails from Jamaica, Haiti, and Martinique.

Much less known and harder to find is a rum relative: *aguardiente de cana*—or cachaça—from Brazil. But seek it out; it is well worth the effort. Once at a Brazilian-themed restaurant in New York City on a torrid Fourth of July, some friends and I were coaxed into ordering a drink made with cachaça: the Caipirinha. A mixture of cachaça, freshly crushed limes, and shaved ice, it is dead easy to make. As the bombs burst around us on our walk home, we felt no fear and certainly marveled at the rockets' red glare.

Tequila

Distilled exclusively in Mexico from the juices of the cactuslike blue agave plant—more commonly called the century plant in the U.S.—tequila boasts origins that are appropriately exotic. Long before the Spanish conquistadors introduced the stills that led to the production of tequila, Mexicans drank a wine made from agave. Perhaps because this mescal wine had been used for centuries in spiritual rites by the Aztec, tequila also became known as an alcohol to be used in rituals. One might say the contemporary practice of shooting shots of tequila with a lick of salt and a lime wedge is a "rite" of sorts, stemming presumably from Mexican machismo (particularly when one shot leads to another and another). Thanks in part to a mistaken association with the hallucinogen mescaline, tequila came to acquire a special cachet among swinging Californians, becoming part of their culture's veneration of native tradition and natural highs.

Tequila comes primarily from only two regions in Mexico: one outside the town of Tequila and the other near Tepatitlán. *Aguamiel*, or honey water, is extracted from the heart of the agave plant and then

distilled twice: once into wine (or mescal) and again to create tequila. Although various agave plants may be used, Mexican law stipulates that tequila must be 51 percent blue-agave-plant distillates, although some say the country's *denominación de origen,* or certification, is enforced none too strictly. Mexico and the U.S., however, do have a treaty that stipulates that tequila not be made north of the border. In exchange, bourbon cannot be produced in Mexico. Both spirits are shipped in large quantities and bottled in both countries. White or silver tequila is aged in wax-lined vats; gold or *añejo* (which literally means old) tequila is aged in oak casks to give it color and body.

No longer the preserve of aging hipsters, tequila seems to be constantly growing in popularity. Margaritas, mixed in a variety of flavors, are largely responsible for this. Like any cocktail worth its salt (in this case, often on the glass's rim), the Margarita has mythical origins. It is said by some to be the invention of North American laborers desperate for a palatable, affordable drink; in one version, Margarita was the local barmaid who assisted in creating it. Or Margarita was the inspiration

for the drink. Or Margarita was the girlfriend of someone essential to its invention. Whatever the truth may
be, according to *Mr. Boston,* Margaritas are now the
third most popular mixed drink at home. But don't take
warnings about tequila's potency with a grain of salt:
you may well find yourself seeing double.

Why does the tropical drink seem to lead so
often toward overindulgent intoxication? I
suppose it's because tropical cocktails are
such unabashedly tasty party drinks. They are colorful,
often sweet (with the occasional sour highlights), and
festive if not downright silly, with their paper parasols
dangling askew from the glass's edge. There will always
be a place for the sublime Sidecar and the glamorous
Gibson. But the drinks and recipes to follow are a joy-
ous celebration of warmer climes and insouciant times.
So move away from the shadowy seriousness of the
Manhattan and Martini, and relax under the sun of the
tropical cocktail. Have fun!